# The Dropshipping buzz

# How to avoid the traps and set up your online shop for drop shipping

# TABLE
# OF
# CONTENTS

# INTRODUCTION

You bought this book because you want to know more about Dropshipping. You want to save time, and, of course, money, but above all, you don't want to lose any! I will tell you of the traps I fell into when I begun my dropshipping journey, and what methods I developed to avoid them. You will not find, in this book, complicated lingo or confusing techniques. Everything will be explained in a short and simple way. I will help you find your "niche" and your Dropshipping supplier.

There are countless Dropshipping suppliers around the world with totally different products, niches and prices. The trick is to know where to find them!

I will show you, among other things, how to legally benefit from Dropshipping, how some Marketplaces might ruin you, how you can avoid waiting for payments to fulfil orders.

I will tell you why use Prestashop rather than Shopify, why I don't use Facebook ads.

I will show you, step by step, what tools you need and how to use them to start your own online business.

Good, now you know what to expect, let's start with the basics.

# WHAT IS

# DROPSHIPPING?

Let's address the heart of the topic : What is "Dropshipping", exactly?

If you ever heard about Dropshipping, it was probably from internet "gurus" or wholesalers themselves advertising this type of service to improve their revenues.

Here is a popular diagram that explains how it works :

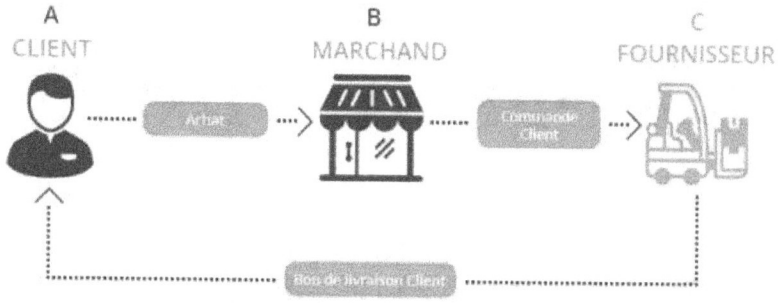

Client A buys a product from merchant B

(you). Merchant B forwards the order to

the supplier or wholesaler C, who then

ships the order directly to the customer.

You received the payment and took care of forwarding the address to the supplier. One crucial part is often left unexplained, and you only realize it later : before supplier C ships the order that you, merchant B, have sold to customer A, you have to buy it first, at the price set by your supplier. This is the point where laws become confusing. We will see that later. It is true that, since you don't keep any inventory reserve, you cannot suffer any loss; this is one of the most popular argument in favour of this sales method, but what they're not telling you, is that you need a seed capital to begin Dropshipping. This seed money must be calculated carefully depending on what you want to sell, and on the frequency of your sales. You aren't in charge of a big company dealing with bulk orders, that can afford to liquidate its stocks at any costs. Your job will be very different : Dropshipping might look like any other import/export business,you have to understand that it is different on several essential points, described in chapter

*Pros and cons of Dropshipping*. Your works consists in planning ahead a sales roadmap and sticking to it : do not sale more than you decided, or you will enter a vicious circle. You must dissociate Dropshipping from the retail : there is not one that is more simple, they are just different from each others, and each method has a set of benefits and drawbacks.

So, why getting involved in Dropshipping?

Because this method allows you to work

for yourself, from the comfort of your home, with a much smaller investment than regular online sales.

In reality, Dropshipping benefits freelancers best, because the margin in Dropshipping can be lower than your PLC competitors (or any other legal entity). Your company's profits after deducing costs constitutes your salary, in a straightforward manner. This isn't the case with a PLC which needs to set a higher margin than yours. As a result, they have to order the same product as you in large quantities to get bulk prices lower than yours.

Dropshipping doesn't suit a large company, see it rather as a springboard. Evolve, build your capital, and start something bigger. Dropshipping is just a start, a way to get some experience in sales and being independent.

Of course you can also establish yourself as a long-term Dropshipper and earn a very decent salary if you don't want to venture further, but Dropshipping offers a plethora of possibilities to creative and willing individuals.

It will be very useful for your next

projects.

# PROS AND CONS OF DROPSHIPPING

Now you have a better idea of what

Dropshipping is, we will see what benefits

it can bring you or what i you need to be

aware of.

We will start with the inconvenients.

As we've seen previously, an

import/export company will  acquire a

large number of mostly foreign products,

to sell them in retail with a profit margin

that can reach up to 300%.

The drawback of using Dropshipping is that, your wholesaler, knowing he will only ever sell you products on a small number basis, will not establish his prices in the same way he would when selling to a retailer. That forces you to lower your profit margin. In most cases, the bare minimum will be 30% of wholesale prices.

Example :

68.00 €

Voir le guide des tailles ›

| TAILLE | DISPONIBILITE | QUANTITE |
|--------|---------------|----------|
| NOSIZE | 2 | − 0 + |

Ajouter au panier

> Description détaillée

Here is a Versace jeans handbag from one of my supplier in clothes and fashion accessories, that I will provide you in chapter *Finding your suppliers*.

We will use prices in Euros for the examples, as it is my most used currency, but of course the methods of calculations and examples that I will provide you work exactly the same way in every currency.

In this example, the buying price for a dropshipper will be 68€. In retail, it will be sold at 204€. Obviously, we cannot sell this product 204€, as internet sales rely mostly on price competition and you will generally find prices much lower than this one.

Sp-stores

Sp-stores Sac à bandoulière nude et doré Versace Jeans - Buzzao

Soyez la première personne à écrire un commentaire sur cet article

Prix EUR 224.40

Nouveau Prix EUR 153.99 **LIVRAISON GRATUITE.**

Economisez EUR 70.41 (31%)

Tous les prix incluent la TVA

Payez cet article en 4 fois

Il ne reste plus que 1 exemplaire(s) en stock.

**Faites-vous livrer entre le 23 et le 27 août** en choisissant la **Livraison Rapide** lors du passage de commande. En savoir plus

Expédié et vendu par Buzzao.

Plus d'articles de Sp-stores ›

Passez la souris sur l'image pour zoomer

On amazon, for example, you can find it for 153.99€ (not including shipping and handling). To the base price of 68, this seller added 125% profit margin. Let's estimate the actual profit this merchant made :

-He sells the handbag for 153.99€

-Amazon's 15% commission amounts to

23.09€

-the merchant then orders the handbag to the supplier for 68€.

-In the end, the merchant will have to add a 13.80% VAT tax (as of 2019, when this book was written) on the 153.99€ sale price, which amounts to 21.25€.

The merchant's benefit after costs will amount to : 41.64€.

Of course, taxes differ, and you will need to get the proper informations about your respective countries.

The trick here, is that laws are still

unclear about Dropshipping, and it's possible to benefit from lower tax rates based on benefits and not overall revenues. We will see that later in chapter **Setting up your company**.

Of course, this is only an example. The seller isn't a dropshipper and his profit margin is therefore superior to what I mentioned above. This is our biggest limitation : profits will always approximate those amounts for a Dropshipper.

The second downside is that you cannot give as much and as detailed informations to your customers as you might want to.

As seller, you are the client's only contact. You are in charge of providing customer service, but you entirely rely on the supplier. When the customer asks a question, you need to forward it to your supplier and wait for him to give you the informations. Communication is one of the most important criterias when choosing your supplier, just after the quality of products and their shipping service.

The third disadvantage of Dropshipping, that I discovered at my own expense, is that synchronizing your stocks from your own shop with marketplaces like Amazon, can be troublesome. If you offer a large variety of products, it might confuse the server and pose problems with your feed aggregator, which is a technology we will detail in *Finding your feed aggregator*.

The feed aggregator will try to gather data on all your products and stocks, but, because of the large quantities, its request will "time out" and won't synchronize your entire stock. The products will be shown as still available, while they are physically out of stock in the suppliers' warehouse. You will be forced to cancel orders, because the products aren't in stock, and will customers will give you negative reviews. On marketplaces, customer feedback is essential. I will show you how you can avoid this type of problem in chapter **_Finding your feed aggregator_** .

The fourth inconvenient is the workload.

You will work alone, in your own house, and, at some point, you might lose track of time. Between new entrances and product pages to set up on different platforms, as, for example, "La Rue du Commerce" (a French-only platform) which demands specific settings for each product, that you have to enter manually. This can be extremely time-demanding when, like me, you have more than 5000 product pages to update, one by one. Some days, it will take all your free time and barely leave any room for hobbies and friends. Before setting your mind on this kind of job, ask yourself if you're ready for this.

Now, let's see the benefits of Dropshipping.

As I told you in the previous chapter, the biggest benefit of Dropshipping is avoiding financial losses. Since you don't keep any stock, your working capital will not suffer a lot of spending without returns at first. This is very convenient with this method : you minimize expenditures to evolve step by step. You do not have to stress out about clearing stocks and unsold goods which can reach astronomical sums, when bad products choices were made. With Dropshipping, you can afford to choose the wrong product because you are just a showcase, your inventory is your supplier's : if a product doesn't sell, you won't lose money. This is why it's best to retrieve your niche's entire listing from your supplier et see what works best. Of course this doesn't mean you won't have any expenditure in the beginning, but they will be minimal, compared to a traditional import/export society. This is also an advantage for a freelancer.

The second advantage of dropshipping relates to stock management, compared with regular companies we'll call "competitors", even though you don't work the same way. When you operate on a Marketplace, like Amazon, you deal with a lot of sellers; some are dropshippers, like you, that you shall be able to identify, and regular retailers. Do not focus on retailers' prices to establish your margin (we will see this in **_"monitoring prices to calculate your profit margin"_** but only on other dropshippers like you, because, when the retailer will have exhausted his limited supply, his customers (whom we will call "prospects")  will naturally flow towards you : they will only have the choice between you and other dropshippers, until the retailer renews its stock, and this is where price will play in the client's choice, provided your delivery times are similar, but, in general, an internet customer is ready to wait longer to pay less, even a just a few euros.

The third, and not least, advantage, is that you can choose a supplier for each country you sell your products in, be it in Europe, USA, or Asia. Regarding marketplaces, you will notice they pay back sales revenues between seven and twenty days after product has been delivered to the client because there is a withdrawal period and return of fourteen days. Thus, Marketplaces are legally bound to honor this period and to keep sales revenues in case of a refund request from the customer. This will not be automatical and you will have to deal with this type of problem with your customer directly on your merchant backoffice. So, in the end, if you are selling from a European supplier in the USA, your delivery time will be a lot longer, and so, will result in a significant delay in the transfer of your sales' revenues. The best way to deal with this problem is to have one or several suppliers for every zones you want to sell your products in. That would be impossible as a regular retailer, as you would ship your products directly from your own warehouse, and, except if you intend to acquire several warehouses in different parts of the world, to bring down delivery times, Dropshipping is the only way to be able selling worldwide with the best delivery times.

# FINDING YOUR "NICHE"

Here we will bring up the "niche" topic.

First of all, what is a "niche"? A niche, is a market targetting specific clients, with specific products, therefore, by targetting specific customers, it will be easier for you to offer products that suit their tastes better. The goal, here, is not to sell anything and everything, as a Marketplace. Of course, you can later open several e-commerce websites, specialised in totally different niches, but to maintain a visual coherence of profesionnal level, you have to separate different product categories in several different shops.

In general, a niche should be something that suits you. For example, if you like fitness or sport in general, you should sell uniquely sport goods; if you like new technologies, you should sell only high tech products. You are a smartphone enthusiast, you get a new one every six months? Then start a smartphone shop.

To summ it up, sell what you know, because it will be easier to ask yourself : "would I buy this product at this price?", "do I find this product appealing?", or, to say it simply, to put yourself in your customer's shoes. But if you have no ideas, I will tell you about an American website famous for connecting retails, or dropshippers, with suppliers. There is a list of suppliers in every domain and specifications that could suit you. It's really the dropshipper's holy Grail. Therefore, during your search, you will be able to

sort out product types, according to the

types of products your suppliers offer,

and, thus, find the niche that suits you.

Here is the link to Salehoo :

https://www.salehoo.com/

Of course, access to the website requires

a fee : for $67 per year, you will have

access to a big list of suppliers based in

every parts of the world, selling different

products. So it's not a useless

investment, because, not only does it

provide you with the suppliers you need,

it can also help you to find your personal

niche.

# MONITORING PRICES TO CALCULATE YOUR PROFIT MARGIN

This step is crucial to plan the budget you will need, to know if you have enough funds for the niche you chose, but, mostly, to set up a sales roadmap, that is to say, the maximum ammount of sales you will be able to fulfill monthly, before having to wait for your sales revenues, to honor your future orders.

A crucial point to avoid the vicious circle I mentioned before, because if your goal is to make the largest number of sales possible in a very short time, you will encounter a problem regarding your working capital : you will have depleted all your cash, and you will be unable to honor your standing orders before your customers have received their products, including customer's withdrawal period, which differs according to Marketplaces. If you do not plan ahead for this, you will be unable to pass on some orders, because you're lacking cash, and you will have to cancel those orders, which brings us back to the problem with bad customer reviews on the Marketplaces. I will never repeat it enough : the reviews from your first customers are of primordial importance in the beginning, because you are new and don't inspire trust. As soon as your first sales are concluded, and your first customers have graded you positively, your sales will multiply. This is why you have to be prepared to avoid those pitfalls from the start.

The method I will give you is pretty simple. Let's take the example of my clothes and fashion accessory provider.

Framed in green you will find the product reference, on each product sheet, you will find its reference, and, sometimes, a barcode (or EAN13) which confirms its authenticity, the fact it's a geniune product from the authentic brand. If you do a google search using this reference, you will find shops, and, sometimes, but, rarely, the product directly on the

Marketplaces, even if, in general,

Marketplaces do not use those

references for Google search engine

optimization.

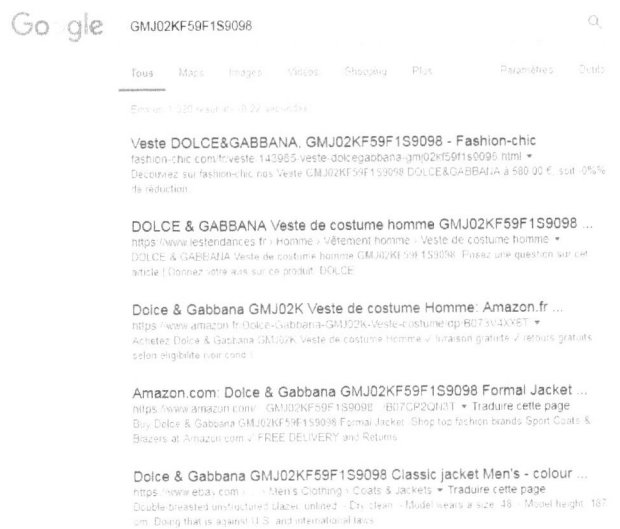

Regarding searching on Amazon, you

can either use the EAN13 code provided

by your supplier, or use the brand name

and a part of the reference. Here is an

example :

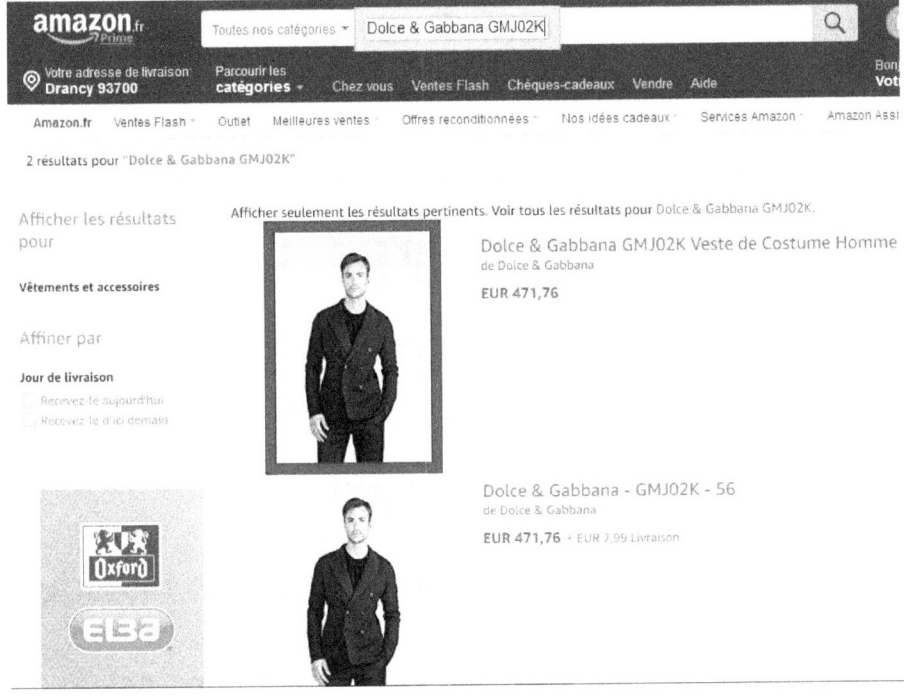

From the search bar, in the green box,

you will find your brand's name and part

of your reference, and, in the blue box,

you will see our Dolce & Gabbana suit

jacket. The lowest price is €471,76 and

€7,99 shipping fees. There is no

difference between this supplier or you, the only difference that can set you appart is the price. Let's do the maths : our suit jacket costs €245 + €6,90 shipping fees on average, our competitor sells it for €471,76, which means he adds a margin ammouting to roughly 90% wholesale price. A 70% margin is a lot more than enough, here, if you want to be noticeably cheaper. This is what we're gonna do. The suit's jacket costs us €245, we will add 70% of this price, €416,50 + €6,90 shipping fees. The total retail price will be €423,40.

Now let's calculate our net benefit :

•Amazon's commission : 15%

•taxes : 23,70% of benefits thanks to the

method we will see in the chapter

**"setting up your company"**

•jacket wholesale price plus shippng fees

: €251,90

net benefit on this sale = €82,39

The first year, you will be exempted from

taxes, in France at least, but many

countries use the same principle to

promote entrepreneurship, so don't

hesitate to get in touch with your local government agencies for more local policies.

Therefore, your net benefit will be €107,99. You will find that, for this type of product, you will have to invest a large part from your working capital, as, in this case, you will need to invest €251,90, to gain €107,99.

Of course, not all products generate as much profit, everything will depend on your competition prices, like the Versace handbang, which generates a net benefit of €41,35.

Using this method of computation, you can find the average, by calculating the maring percentage on part of your products. Example : 125% (handbag) + 70% (jacket) ÷ 2 = 97,5%. So we will round down our profit margin to 95%.

# FINDING YOUR

# SUPPLIERS

In this chapter, we will see how you will find your suppliers.

First, I will provide you two of my personal suppliers, in case you might be interested in selling clothes and fashion accessories, or consumer electronics.

The first one, is an European supplier, based in Italy, named Brandsditrbution.

You can find them here :

https://www.brandsdistribution.com/

Their dropshipping service includes a monthly subscription to use their services. Not all providers require a subscription to use their service, but this one has an extensive platform with a lot of brand name products, with a high quality, proprietary, shipping service. Their customer service is also very good. You won't find better amongst fashion suppliers. They ship almost everywhere in Europe, and, recently, they started shipping to the USA and Canada as well.

They offer 3 formulas :

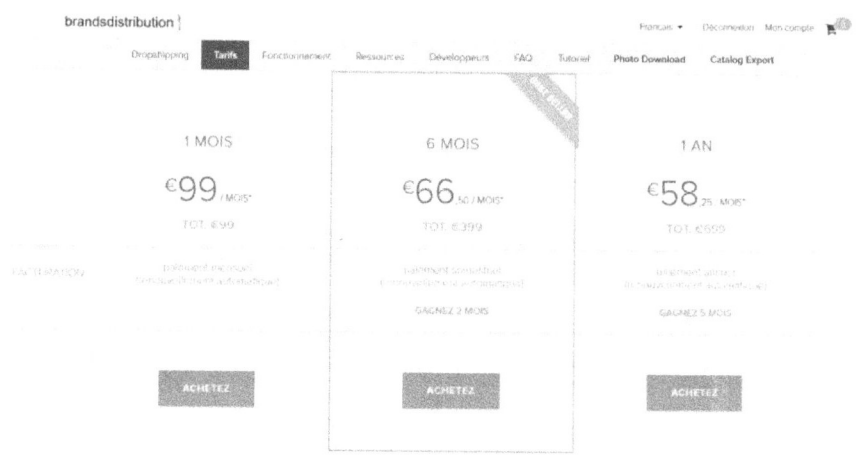

I have to suggest you the 6 months

formula which is perfect for a start.

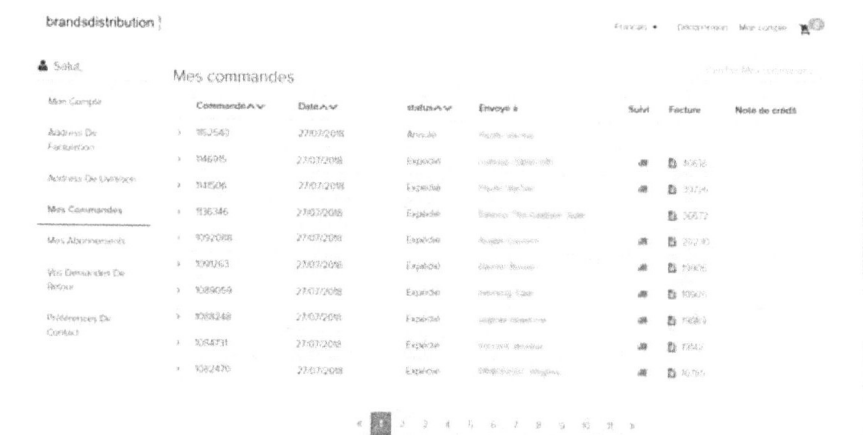

This will be the interface you will use to

follow your orders, with the dedicated shipping tracker, to be able to inform your clients. The rest is as simple as ordering a product online on any website, you will only have to fill your client's name and adress as recipient of the package.

Now let's move to the second supplier which is based in Spain. Bigbuy offers high quality services and products. It provides a large array of products, but I suggest you to limit yourself to consumer electronics, as shipping fees are very high for bulky products. You can check their website here :

https://www.bigbuy.eu/fr/

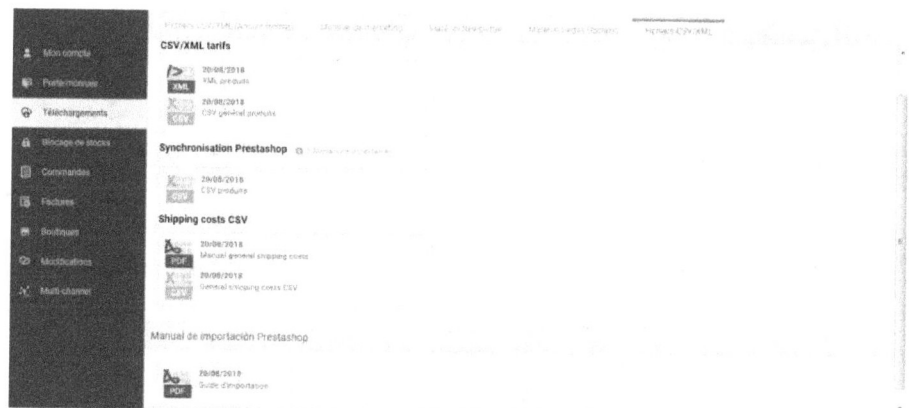

You will find in this section everything you need to import your products in your shop manually.

Activez le pack grossiste qui s'adapte le mieux à votre entreprise

Bigbuy also offers 3 packs, the best one for you will be the middle one, for 139€ the first month, then 49€ per month to use this supplier's dropshipping service. Those two suppliers have their own stock synchronisation and product importation modules, in case you would want to

automatize this, and I highly advise you to. It's a very useful one-time investment : you will work alone, and this type of automatization will save you a lot of time and work, especially if computers aren't your specialty.

We will see that more in detail in *"setting up your shop with Prestashop"*.

Now you have your first two suppliers, but should they not suit your needs, then, as I explained in chapter *"pros and cons of Dropshipping"*, one of the biggest advantages is that you can ship your products worldwide, by picking your suppliers by market zone and country by best delivery times.

We will use the SaleHoo that I mentioned in chapter *"find your niche"*. As a reminder, subscription to Salehoo is only 67$ per year, but there's better : if you aren't entirely satisfied of the services they offer, you are elligible for a full refund. You have nothing to lose and everything to gain.

Here is the link to Salehoo :

https://www.salehoo.com/

# SETTING UP YOUR

# SHOP WITH PRESTASHOP

Now we are entering in the technical phase of the preparation, this chapter will be entirely dedicated to the creation of your store, we will see a lot of key points to handle the "prestashop" solution.

First of all, why Prestashop? You surely

heard a lot about Shopify, which is technically more interesting than Prestashop, especially regarding shop management, which is extremely simple, because you don't need any technical knowledge. But there is a problem, which is, of course, the monthlee fee. The only thing that justifies those fees, is the user-friendliness. And, of course, the more products you have, the more you need performance, and the more expensive it gets. In my opinion, this is waste of cash, compared to Prestashop, which is free.

When you're willing to learn, and eager to succeed, you don't want to choose the easy road. You will have to, like me, learn to create your shop step by step and use it. This book isn't dedicated only to using Prestashop, you will only learn the basics and installation of what we call a "CMS", which prestashop is.

Later, you will be free to advance your knowledge of Prestashop with tutorials that can be found easily on internet. It is very user-friendly and you will find your way around quickly.

To start off, you will need to find a domain name. This will be your shop's name. As soon as you've settled for one, you can move to the next step.

Second step : pick a web-hosting provider. I recommend OVH, the one I use myself. Here is their link : ttps://www.ovh.com/fr/hebergement-web/hebergement-pro.xml it is a direct link to the subscription package which fits your needs best, currently for 7,19€ TTC per month. When you click on "order", you will have the option to choose your domain name, as below. You will have to

add a fee, renewable every year. Of

course it will have to be "available" and

not "transferable".

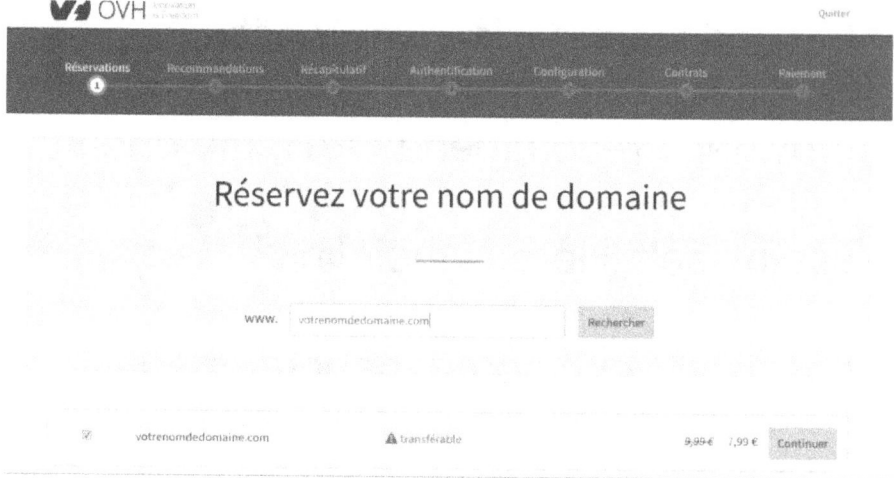

You will then have to choose the service :

as you will see on the description, for

you, the most appropriated one will be

the gold service.

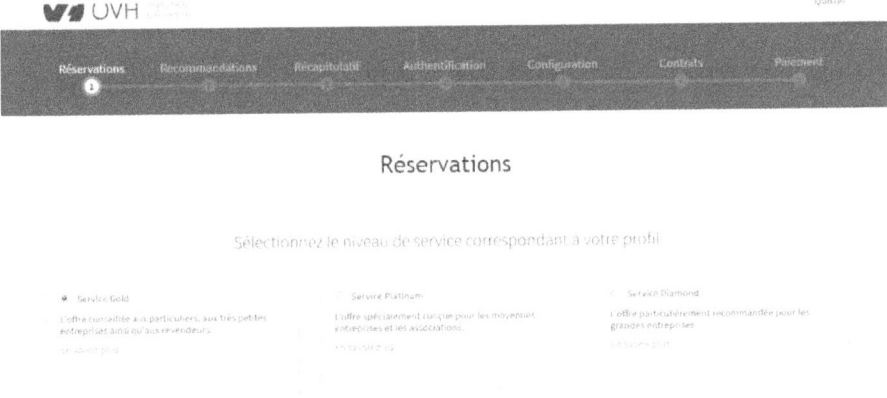

With OVH, creating your hosting platform is directly integrated into the Prestashop module, pre-installed, which will break the back of the work for you. Saving time is a must. Pick the Prestashop module as shown below :

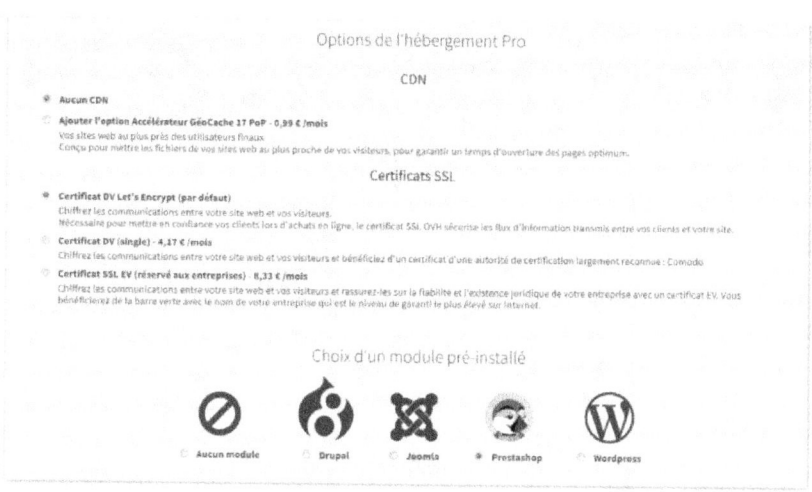

Then proceed with payment, and you will

be able to access your hosting platform.

This is what your client interface will look

like, with OVH.

"Launch the automated installer"

To access it, you will just have to fill in your website's url, that is, your domain name.

Now let 's talk see the installation of Prestashop itself.

Prestashop's automated intaller makes set up relatively simple : just a few minutes will suffice. Make sure you read ever page carefully so you do not miss any information. To launch the installer, just browse to Prestashop's directory on your web server (which should be the url of your domain name), and the script will automatically detect that Prestashop is missing, and will direct you to the automated installer. At the same time, the prestashop.zip file you uploaded will be unpacked, except if that file was pre-installed by OVH, which is the case here. Now, all the Prestashop files are available on your web server. From there on, all the Prestashop files are available on your web server. All you have to do is reading, clicking and filing up a few forms.

There are six steps. On the top of the page, the installation wizard will point your current evolution in the process : grey circles become green checks once a step is completed.

Step 1 : welcome page

This page is a quick presentation of the installation process. You can choose the language in which instructions will appear.

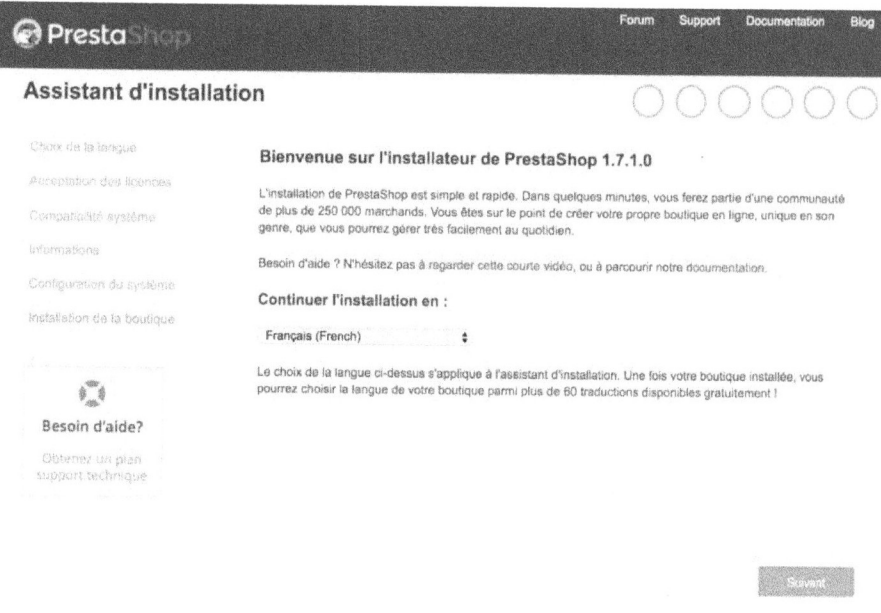

You also have a link to the documentation page (http://doc.prestashop.com/) and a link to the support. To know more about Prestashop's support, go to http://support.prestashop.com/fr/. Select your language, then click on "next". This step will allow you to define Prestashop's default language, but you can also activate other languages as well.

Step 2 : Prestashop licenses

This second page states a simple condition : Prestashop is free and distributed as a set of open source licenses. You cannot use this program if you do not accept the licenses' conditions. In this step, you will have to clearly accept those conditions. You can read Prestashop : Open Software

License 3.0's condition on this page :

http://www.opensource.org/licenses/OSL-

3.0.  The conditions for using Academic

Free License 3.0 (add-ons and themees)

are available here :

http://opensource.org/licenses/AFL-3.0.

## Acceptation des licences

Afin de profiter gratuitement des nombreuses fonctionnalités qu'offre PrestaShop, merci de prendre connaissance des termes des licences ci-dessous. Le coeur de PrestaShop est publié sous licence O' 3.0 tandis que les modules et thèmes sont publiés sous licence AFL 3.0.

### Core: Open Software License ("OSL") v. 3.0

This Open Software License (the "License") applies to any original work of authorship (the "Original Work") whose owner (the "Licensor") has placed the following licensing notice adjacent to the copyright notice for the Original Work:

**Licensed under the Open Software License version 3.0**

1. Grant of Copyright License. Licensor grants You a worldwide, royalty-free, non-exclusive, sublicensable license, for the duration of the copyright, to do the following:

☑ J'accepte les termes et conditions du contrat ci-dessus.

Précédent                                                                 Suivant

You will have to accept both of them to install Prestashop.

To reach the next step you will have to check "I accept those conditions", then click on "next". If you do not accept them, you will not be able to install Prestashop. You will not even be able to click on "next".

Step 3 and 4 : system compatibility and shop's informations.

The third page consists in a quick test of all the server's parameters. In most cases you won't ever see it. Indeed, if no error is yound, you will be immediately redirected to the fourth step : "shop's informations". You will still be able to view the third page by clicking on "system compatibility", located on the left side bar. If an error is found during the test, the installer will show the "system compatibility" page, with every verification that failed.

System compatibility

This page allows you to check that your server's configuration is correct : PHP parameters, files and directories permissions, third party tools, etc.

Nous vérifions en ce moment la compatibilité de PrestaShop avec votre système

Si vous avez la moindre question, n'hésitez pas à visiter notre documentation et notre forum communautaire.

✓ La compatibilité de PrestaShop avec votre système a été vérifiée

Rafraîchir ces informations

Précedent

Suivant

Shop information

This is where you can start customizing

your shop : by giving it a name, indicating

its core business, and filing up the shop

owner's personal details (which implies

legal obligations in most countries). Do not add the colon (":") to your shop's name, that might disrupt some functionalities (sending e-mails, for example). You can replace the colon by a dash, if you want two parts in the title. For example, write "Myshop-the best shop to buy" instead of "My shop : the best shop to buy".

## Informations à propos de votre boutique

| | |
|---|---|
| Nom de la boutique | ps171 |
| Activité principale | Merci de choisir une activité ▾ |

*Aidez-nous à mieux vous connaître pour que nous puissions vous orienter et vous proposer les fonctionnalités les plus adaptées à votre activité !*

| | |
|---|---|
| Installer les produits de démo | ● Oui ○ Non |

*Les produits de démo sont un bon moyen pour apprendre à utiliser PrestaShop. Vous devriez les installer si vous n'êtes pas familier avec le logiciel.*

| | |
|---|---|
| Pays | France ▾ |

## Votre compte

| | |
|---|---|
| Prénom | Jean |
| Nom | Petit |
| Adresse e-mail | jean@prestashop.com |

*• Cette adresse e-mail vous servira d'identifiant pour accéder à l'interface de gestion de votre boutique.*

| | |
|---|---|
| Mot de passe | •••••••• |

*• Minimum 8 caractères*

| | |
|---|---|
| Confirmation du mot de passe | •••••••• |

Les informations recueillies font l'objet d'un traitement informatique et statistique, elles sont nécessaires aux membres de la société PrestaShop afin de répondre au mieux à votre demande. Ces informations peuvent être communiquées à nos partenaires à des fins de prospection commerciale et être transmises dans le cadre de nos relations partenariales. Conformément à la loi « Informatique et Libertés » du 6 janvier 1978 modifiée en 2004, vous pouvez exercer votre droit d'accès, de rectification et d'opposition au traitement des données qui vous concernent en cliquant ici.

Précédent        Suivant

This is also the step where you will

choose the password you'll use to log-in to your shop administration panel. Make sure to pick it carefully, so you can both remember it without too much efforts, but it is also secured enough. Then click on "next".

Step 5 : Setting up the system

This page countains a form allowing you to indicate to Prestashop the location of your database, and which datas to use, as well as a few other details. In theory, your web host, OVH, has already given you all those details.

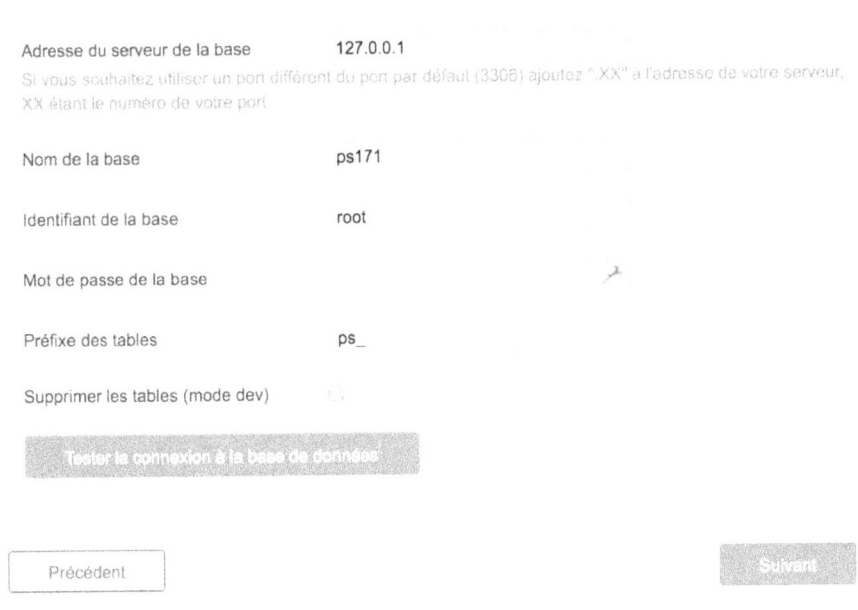

**Configurez la connexion à votre base de données en remplissant les champs suivants.**

Pour utiliser PrestaShop vous devez créer une base de données afin d'y enregistrer toutes les données nécessaires au fonctionnement de votre boutique.
Veuillez compléter les champs ci-dessous pour connecter PrestaShop à votre base de données.

Adresse du serveur de la base          127.0.0.1

Si vous souhaitez utiliser un port différent du port par défaut (3306) ajoutez ".XX" a l'adresse de votre serveur, XX étant le numéro de votre port

Nom de la base          ps171

Identifiant de la base          root

Mot de passe de la base

Préfixe des tables          ps_

Supprimer les tables (mode dev)

Tester la connexion à la base de données

Précédent          Suivant

Fill in all fields, by indicating your login

details to the database, provided by the

host :

**database adress :** this is the name of

your MySQL host. It can be associated ot

your domain name (as

[http://sql.exemple.com](http://sql.exemple.com)) or to your host

(as http://mysql2.alwaysdata.com),  or it

can be just an IP adress (like

46.105.78.185).

**Database name** : this is the name of the

database you want Prestashop to store

datas in. It can be an existing database

on your MySQL server, or a database you

created with the help of phpMyAdmin (or

any other SQL tool), in the section

"Creating a database for your shop" of

this guide.

**Log in details** : this MySQL username to access your database.

**Database password** : this is the password to your MySQL user.

**Database engine :** your database engine is the heart of your database server. InnoDB is the default engine. I recommend using it, even if some advanced users will opt for another engine.

As a rule of thumb it's not necessary to modify default parameters.

**Tables prefix** : This is the prefix your

base data tables will use. The default setting is "ps_", which prints Prestashop's SQL tables like "ps_cart" or "ps_customer". If you need to install several instances of Prestashop on the same database, you will have to use a different prefix for each installation. I recommend you to create a separate database for each Prestashop installation, as long as your internet provider allows it. Even better : install Prestashop only once, and activate the multishop option, so you can manage several shops from the same admin panel, in Prestashop.

**Tables suppression option** : this option is only available in developer mode. When you re-install Prestashop, you can choose to delete existing Prestashop data tables and start over from scractch. Clik on "test connection to the database", to confirm the server details are correct. Click on "next" : the installation starts with your shop's configuration, filling up your database tables, etc. This operation can take a few minutes : please be patient and do not touch your browser!

The installer will proceed as follow :

-Creation of the file setting.inc.php with

your parameters.

-Creation of the database tables.

-Creation of the default shop, with default

languages.

-Fill up your database tables.

-Configuration of your shop's details.

-Installation of default modules.

-Installation of display datas (products, categories, users, CMS pages etc...).

-Installation of the theme.

Once this step is over, your shop if installed, ready to be configured.

 Finishing the installation

As you can read on the last page of the installation process, you will have a last few actions to perform before quitting the installer.

**L'installation est finie !**

Vous venez d'installer votre boutique en ligne, merci d'avoir choisi PrestaShop !

Merci de conserver les informations de connexion suivantes :

Email                jean@prestashop.com

Mot de passe        ********** (Affichage)

🖨 Imprimer cette page

Pour des raisons de sécurité, vous devez supprimer le dossier "install" manuellement. ❓

**Administration**

*Accédez dès à présent à votre interface de gestion pour commencer la configuration de votre boutique.*

Gérez votre boutique

**Front-Office**

*Découvrez l'apparence de votre boutique avec quelques produits de démonstration, prête à être personnalisée par vos soins !*

Découvrez votre boutique

To easily buff up your installation's security, delete some important files and folders. This operation is done using an FTP client, directly on the server. Delete the following files :

-"install" directory (essential)

-"/docs" folder (optional), unless you need to test the importation tool with the file templates located in this folder.

Click on "managing your shop" to reach the admin panel.

Do not forget to add the administrator's connexion address to your bookmarks.

Congratulations ! The installation is now complete.

Now, we will proceed to install what we call "modules", on Prestashop. These are your supplier's modules to automatize your products' importation and your shop's stocks. Regarding the first

supplier, Brandsdistribution, you will have

to create an account on their partner's

website : https://shop.zero11.it/ .

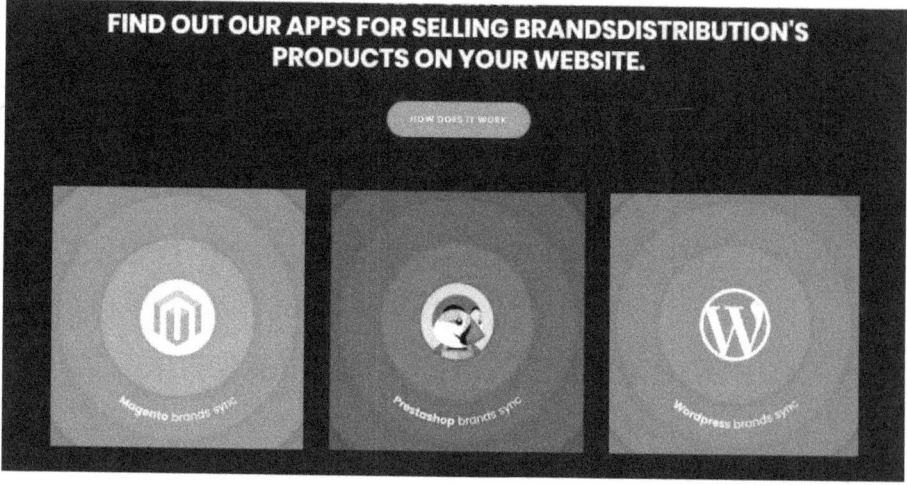

Click on "Prestashop brands sync" :

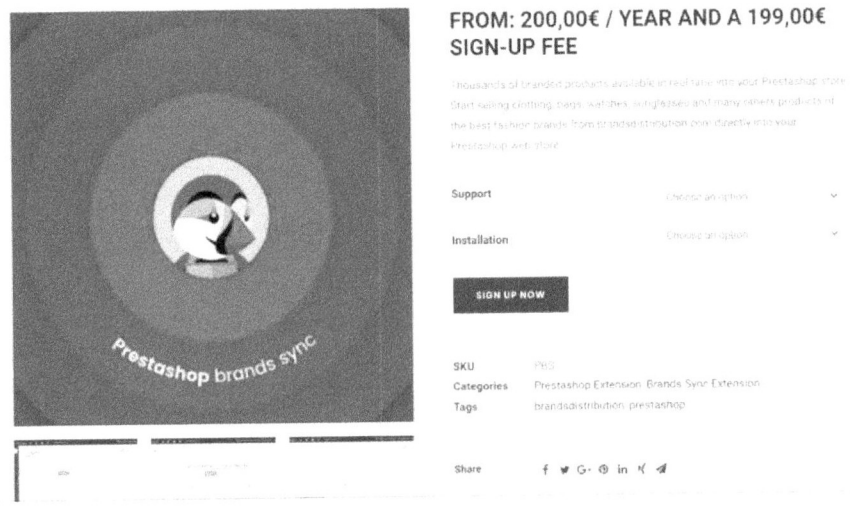

**FROM: 200,00€ / YEAR AND A 199,00€
SIGN-UP FEE**

Thousands of branded products available in real time into your Prestashop store. Start selling clothing, bags, watches, sunglasses and many others products of the best fashion brands from a dedistribution.com directly into your Prestashop web store.

Support                    Choose an option              ∨

Installation               Choose an option              ∨

**SIGN UP NOW**

SKU            PHS
Categories     Prestashop Extension, Brands Sync Extension
Tags           brandsdistribution, prestashop

Share          f � G· ⊕ in ⋉ ⫪

you will be directed to this page

describing the product. The module costs

399€ overall, but it will be available to

download for free and without limits

during the first year, then you will have to

pay the fee to renew it. Fortunately, you

won't have to, because it will keep

functioning  as long as you don't uninstall

it from your computer or your Prestashop

database.

## MY ACCOUNT

| Dashboard | | Product | Downloads remaining | Expires | Download |
|---|---|---|---|---|---|
| Orders | | Prestashop Brands Sync - No, No | | Never | ps-brandssync |
| Subscriptions | | | | | |
| Downloads | ⬇ | | | | |
| Addresses | | | | | |
| Account details | | | | | |
| Logout | | | | | |

For any technical questions please send email to
brandsdistribution-helpdesk@zero11.it
our ticketing system so you can follow status and we can track and solve easily all customers requests.

On your Zero11 account, you will be able

to download the module, by clicking on

"ps-brandsync", then you will have to log-

in on your admin panel, in Prestashop.

We well call it "back-office".

Fill in the email used to install Prestashop

and your

password.

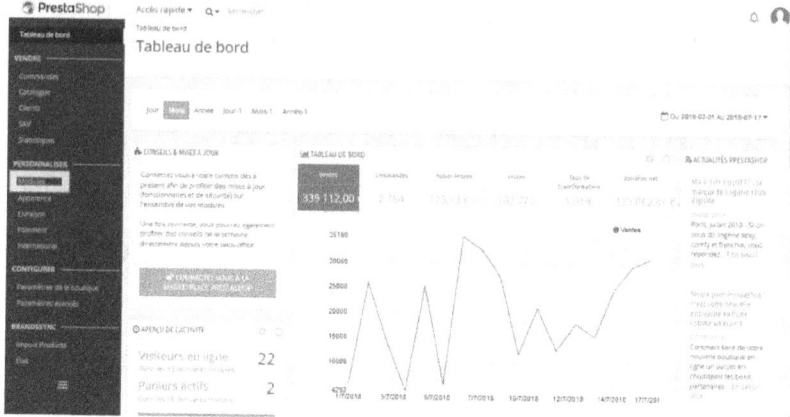

Go to "modules"

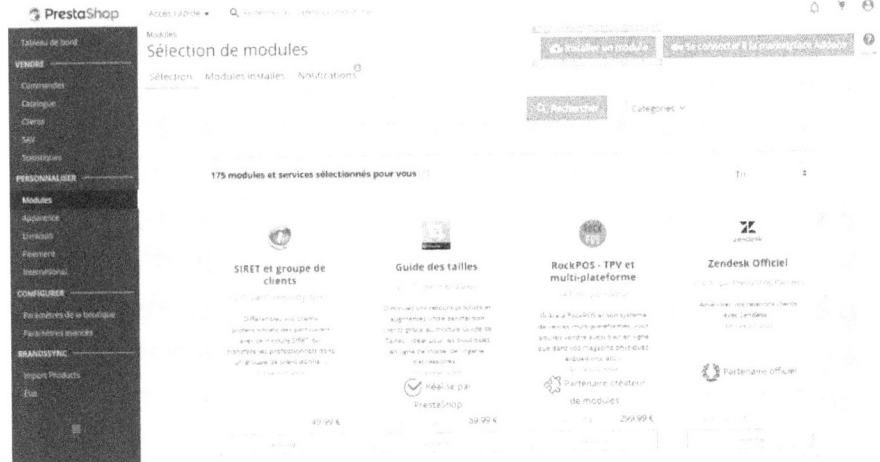

Then "installing a module"

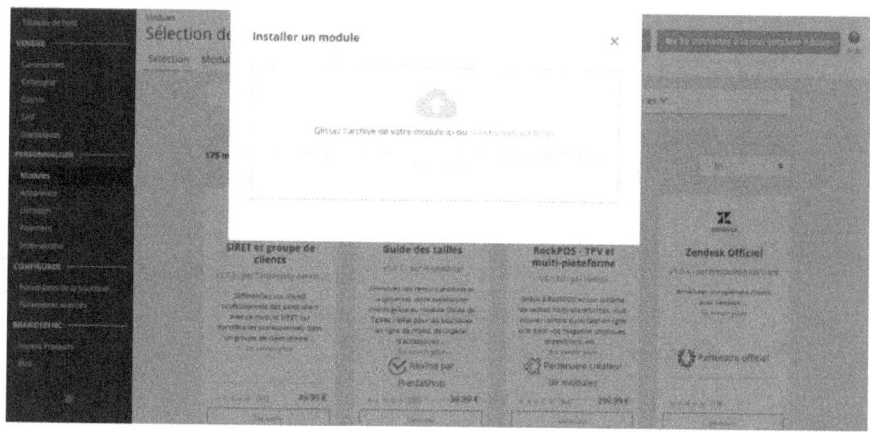

Select the zip file you downloaded earlier

from Zero11 and install the module.

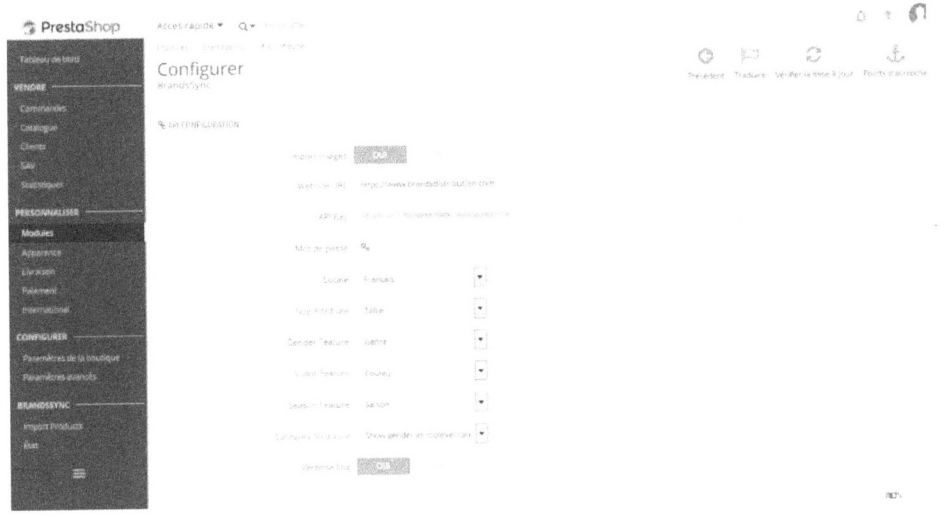

Go to "installed modules", and configure

Brandsync. In "website's url", indicate

Brandsdistribution's url, as shown above,

and fill in the API Key. It will be provided

by your supplier by email, on your

request, after you signed up and

suscribed to one of its three Dropshipping

service plans.

Then configure your VAT rate, and the

benefit margin to apply to your imported

products.

Next, you will have to configure a "cron

task" : this is an automated task, that will

execute a specific request on your server.

You can use the OVH's one, directly from

your interface, on your OVH account, but

I recommend opting for Easycron. Here is the link to their website : https://www.easycron.com.

You can register for free and create free cron tasks.

All you will have to do is input your module « `http(s)://<votre-domaine>/modules/brandssync/cron.php` ». Replace "your domain" with the name of your shop, which should be your domain name. E.g. :

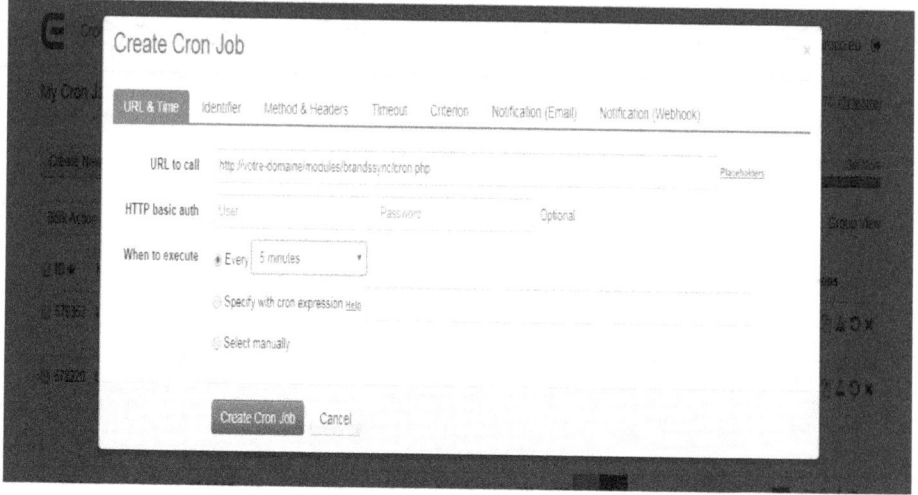

Make sure to set the delay between each request to five minutes, so your stock gets updated at this frequency.

Click on "create cron job" and your task will proceed normally. Subsequently, you will have to start choosing the products you want to import.

You will have a large choice of clothes and fashion accessories of several brands to import. All you will have to do is select the ones you prefer, or import the entire catalog. From there onwards, everything will proceed automatically :

when an order is placed on your shop, it will be automatically forwarded to your supplier, who will set aside the product for you, for up to three days, until you pay the invoice.

Now, concerning the BigBuy's supplier module, the process will be mostly similar. The only thing that changes will be the acquisition mode of the module, that you will find, this time, in Prestashop addons. This is a sort of marketplace dedicated to Prestashop modules. On this platform, you will find a lot of

modules that will be useful later, when

you've earned some experience in online

sale, and you know which modules suit

your needs best.

Here is the link to the site :

https://addons.prestashop.com/fr/

You will just have to type "Bigbuy" in the

search bar and buy the one highlighted in

green. The price including taxes will be 299.99€. But, once more, the time and energy you will save will be tremendous. It is a one-time investment you will not have to repeat. As I told you, the investment is negligible compared with an import/export society, but investment is essential to succeed.

Now, to install the modue, you will just have to use the same method as the Brandssync module, it works the same way. Categories will create themselves as products are imported.

Your shop is now ready to use!

Of course, you will have to improve the visual aspect of your shop, specify the general terms and conditions and your return policy (it will be the same as your supplier's).

Even if, at this point, your shop is, in reality, just a gateway to the Marketplaces, we will not pay to acquire prospects, but instead begin straight away with sales on Marketplaces, so we can later invest in traffic acquisition. It is essential to start generating revenues before moving to marketing, that will not convert to cash before several months. There is nothing better than Marketplaces : you do not bring the customers to you, you go to them.

# SETTING UP YOUR

# COMPANY

Now that your shop is ready to sale products, it also has to be compliant with the law. There is nothing more simple : register as an "auto-entrepreneur".

A lot of online companies can help those who cannot do it themselves, but I believe it is a waste of money. There is nothing difficult in registering your independent business. We will also discuss the topic of reducing taxes on benefits, in a legal way.

We will detail the steps required in France to get registered as an "auto-entrepreneur". It will be different according to the country you reside in, but it will still be helpful as the procedures are very similar.

To begin, go to :

https://www.cfe.urssaf.fr/autoentrepreneu r/CFE_Bienvenue

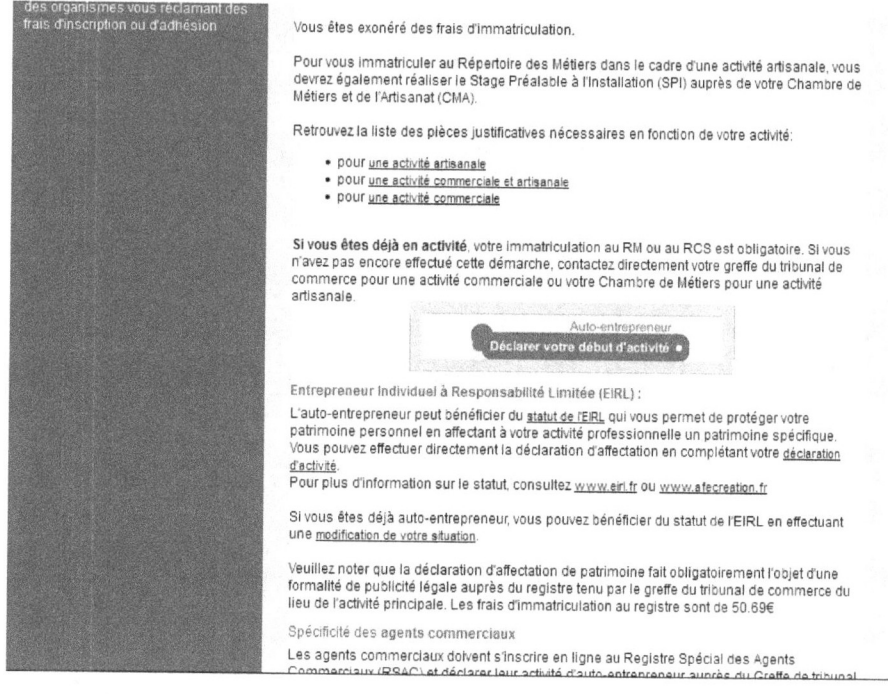

des organismes vous réclamant des frais d'inscription ou d'adhésion

Vous êtes exonéré des frais d'immatriculation.

Pour vous immatriculer au Répertoire des Métiers dans le cadre d'une activité artisanale, vous devrez également réaliser le Stage Préalable à l'Installation (SPI) auprès de votre Chambre de Métiers et de l'Artisanat (CMA).

Retrouvez la liste des pièces justificatives nécessaires en fonction de votre activité:

- pour une activité artisanale
- pour une activité commerciale et artisanale
- pour une activité commerciale

**Si vous êtes déjà en activité**, votre immatriculation au RM ou au RCS est obligatoire. Si vous n'avez pas encore effectué cette démarche, contactez directement votre greffe du tribunal de commerce pour une activité commerciale ou votre Chambre de Métiers pour une activité artisanale.

Auto-entrepreneur
Déclarer votre début d'activité •

Entrepreneur Individuel à Responsabilité Limitée (EIRL) :

L'auto-entrepreneur peut bénéficier du statut de l'EIRL qui vous permet de protéger votre patrimoine personnel en affectant à votre activité professionnelle un patrimoine spécifique. Vous pouvez effectuer directement la déclaration d'affectation en complétant votre déclaration d'activité.
Pour plus d'information sur le statut, consultez www.eirl.fr ou www.afecreation.fr

Si vous êtes déjà auto-entrepreneur, vous pouvez bénéficier du statut de l'EIRL en effectuant une modification de votre situation.

Veuillez noter que la déclaration d'affectation de patrimoine fait obligatoirement l'objet d'une formalité de publicité légale auprès du greffe du registre tenu par le greffe du tribunal de commerce du lieu de l'activité principale. Les frais d'immatriculation au registre sont de 50.69€

Spécificité des agents commerciaux

Les agents commerciaux doivent s'inscrire en ligne au Registre Spécial des Agents Commerciaux (RSAC) et déclarer leur activité d'auto-entrepreneur auprès du Greffe du tribunal

You will just have to click on the zone squared in green and follow the steps to register online. Later, you will need to get an ACCRE form to send under 45 days to avoid taxes, if you are elligible to the exemption for unemployed persons creating or buying a company. As I explained earlier, this kind of programs, supporting entrepreneurs who open a business, exist in a large number of countries and it is important you seek informations for the one you are interested in.

As soon as you will receive the clerk's reply by post, your K-bis extract with your SIRET number, you can begin selling. All you will need to do as an auto-entrepreneur to comply with the law, is to keep records of your purchases and sales. All the products you bought, the prices you paid for them and how much you sold them for.

Regarding taxes, you will find everything you need on the web portal for auto-entrepreneur of the country you settled for. Here is what the page, used to declare our benefits, looks like, in france :

As a trader, you should have to declare your sales revenue as "ventes de marchandises" (sale of goods), but that would make you pay way too much taxes, while your benefit margin is smaller than a retailer.

Technically and legally, you aren't "selling online" yourself, you are a bridge between the supplier and the customer. The supplier mandates you to buy a product to the consumer, you are therefore considered as a "prestataire de services commerciaux" (provider of commercial services). Taxes will therefore not be calculated based on your revenues, but only based on your benefits. Your benefits will become your revenues and this is where you will save money.

Let's take an example :

You sell a product for 125€ that you bought for 60€. Normally, as a retailer, you should declare 125€ and pay 17.25€ on this transaction, but, as a service provider, you will only pay taxes on your benefits, so the ammount you pay will only be 15.40€. On an annual basis, the ammount you will save is not marginal at all, especially when you will have to reduce your margin because one of your competitor set their prices very low. When you have to lower your margin on a product because of a competitor, if you don't opt for declaring your taxes that way, you will simply lose money, because calculating them based on revenues doesn't take into acount your margin but only the price you sold the product for. Prestashop will create the invoices for you. What you will need is to create a folder with a different sub-folder for each month, in which you will transfer the invoices from your customers and suppliers. Print them and store them in a binder, each invoice matched with its unique customer, so it will be easier to sort out during your quaterly or monthly bookkeeping.

# SPREADING UP TO

# MARKETPLACES

This is where things really start. Your first

sales will occur on marketplaces, in

particular, Amazon, because thanks to a

monthly fee ammounting to about 40€,

you will have access to customers all

across Europe. This is where our capital

will increase and will gradually open up to

other Marketplaces, like Cdiscount or

Rue du Commerce, in France, or other

Marketplaces according to the country you chose to sell to.

Why not start with all of them at once? Well it's because Cdiscount will pay you only two months after your first sales, in the best scenario, and you cannot afford to lend money for two months to pay for your products, when you start. Other Marketplaces in other countries works similarly, and you could receive the proceeds from the sales, at most one month after the first sale, as Amazon does. Regarding Rue du Commerce, as I told you, some Marketplaces require a lot more details on your products and you will have to fill them manually, which will be very time-consuming. If you are selling on Amazon during this time, it will motivate you to continue, because it is not the most fun of tasks. To that end, you will need either a feed aggregator that will charge per month, like Iziflux (the one I'm using in France) or a module that you will find in Prestashop addons as I mentioned in the chapter "setting up your shop with Prestashop". You will only have to type in the search bar : "amazon", "cdiscount", or "rue du commerce" and you will find what you are looking for, for a price, but a one-time fee unlike feed aggregators. However, feed aggregators offer training to learn how to use them, as Iziflux does. You will find this module in Prestashop addons, for free, but it will only work with an Iziflux membership. If you contact them, they will offer to call you for free to discuss your needs and explain what they can offer you.

Or you can look for a feed aggregator

located in your country, or one that offers an English-speaking customer service.

Installing those modules is done the same way as with the modules used to import products from suppliers Brandsdistribution and Bigbuy.

Now we will start getting registered on Amazon. To do that, you will need to follow one of those links :

NORTH AMERICA :

USA :https://services.amazon.com/

CANADA :

https://www.amazon.ca/b/?node=136534

59011&ref=as_u s_header_ca-

flag&Id=SCSOAlogin

MEXICO :

https://services.amazon.com.mx/

SOUTH AMERICA :

Brazil :

https://services.amazon.com.br/venda-

na- amazon.html

EUROPE :

UK : https://services.amazon.co.uk/

FR : https://services.amazon.fr/

DE : https://services.amazon.de/

ES : https://services.amazon.es/

IT : https://services.amazon.it/

ASIA :

INDIA :

https://services.amazon.in/home/internati

onal- sellers.htm

CHINA : https://kaidian.amazon.cn/

JAPAN : https://services.amazon.co.jp/

KOREA : https://services.amazon.co.kr/

THAILAND :

https://services.amazon.co.th/

SINGAPORE :

https://services.amazon.com.sg/

OCEANIA :

Australia :

https://services.amazon.com.au/

Now click on "start selling", then you will

be redirected on the connexion page.

Click on "create your Amazon account".

Créer un compte

Votre nom

E-mail

Mot de passe

Les mots de passe doivent au moins avoir 6 caractères.

Entrez le mot de passe à nouveau

Saisissez les caractères que vous voyez

**g27gd3**

Saisissez les caractères suivants

Suivant

After you've finished creating your

account, you will reach a page where all

informations about your company,

especially your trade register numer,

which is your SIREN number, in France,

or your company registration number in

other countries, will be needed.

Amazon will verify that all your informations are correct, and will keep your updated when you can start selling, by email.

With other Marketplaces, steps will be mostly the same, excepted for Rue du Commerce, that will require you to sign a contract on paper and to send them by post. This can happen in other countries as well.

# ESTIMATING YOUR

# BUDGET

Thanks to the method to calculate the margin, given in chapter "monitoring prices to calculate your profit margin", you are now able to know your initial investment.

In the situation where you couldn't invest the ammount indicated for your niche, it woul be preferable to pick up a less expensive niche , thanks to Salehoo.

For example, let's consider our Versace Jeans handbag and our suit jacket from Dolce & Gabbana :

(125% for the handbag + 70% for the suit jacket)÷2=97.5%.

We will round up our margin to 95%.

Now let's set a goal for our monthly sales, knowing that our benefits as an auto-entrepreneur are capped at 70 000€ in France, which ammounts to 5833€ of monthly benefits before taking off 23.70% (make sure to seek out the correct ammounts if you sell in a different country).

Of course you will not reach this level in the first months, so let's set our limit to half of this, which Is 2411€. To calculate your investment to earn 2411€, we need your margin percentage, which is 95%, calculated from our two products. Of course you will need to use a lot more products to calculate your exact margin. I personally recommend around a hundred products. You will need to invest 2538€ to gain 95% more, 2411€. Your total monthly sales will therefore have to ammount to 4949€. 4949€ - 2538€ (cost price of your products) = 2411€ (your benefit)

If you cannot afford to invest 2538€ monthly (knowing those funds will come back to you a month later with a 2411€ benefit), you might need to think about choosing a less expensive niche. It is that simple.

Of course, you will have to add to this, fixed costs paid before sales can begin, such as the monthly professional seller fees, on Amazon, modules to import products from your suppliers to your

shop, the module needed to import your

shop on Amazon (if you do not opt for the

feed aggregator on a monthly fee), and,

of course, the subscription to

Dropshipping services.

# FINDING YOUR

# FEED

# AGGREGATOR

In this chapter, we will talk about the feed

aggregator, especially Iziflux, the one I'm

using myself.

This tool will allow you to export your

products on a plethora of Marketplaces,

directly from one platform. This is

otherwise impossible because you will

always have to use a module specifically crated for a Marketplace. This is a choice to make according to your likings : one monthly fee to access several Marketplaces and platforms (Google shopping included), or a one-time fixed cost for all the different Marketplaces on which you want to sell.

I will give you the link to Iziflux which is a French company, so you can contact them and learn more about their services and prices, depending on your total number of products, then make your own choice : https://www.iziflux.com/

You will find here two other links for international feed aggregator with an English-speaking customer service :

Lengow : https://www.lengow.com/

Magnalister:

https://www.magnalister.com/en/

Now let's put that aside and address the issue of stock syncrhonization and server "time-out" when you have too many products, or synchronizations aren't fast enough, which is the case with Iziflux, which cannot, as your shop does, update your stocks in the Marketplace, every five minutes. In this case, we will use a simple method : creating export rules. That means, when your quantities will reach a certain ammount, the feed aggregator will indicate that your product is out of stock on the Marketplace. This will prevent the product being synchronized too late on the Marketplace when it's really out of stock. I suggest to set this ammount below 5. As soon as the product will reach a quantity below five, it will be automatically set to zero and the product will not be available for sale. The method will be the same with export modules towards Amazon, that you will find on pestashop addons, if you do not opt for a feed aggregator.

From now on, everything is in place to start selling your products. You have your supplier, your shop, your company has been registered, you set up your professionnal account on Amazon and exported your products using the feed aggregator or a module.

Now you're gonna start receiving

orders.During the first months, you will have to remain at this level and not go too fast. Later, you will open another professional seller account on another Marketplace, then another. You have to obtain good ratings and visibility. From here onwards, we can really invest in our personnal shop, where 15% of your sales will not be transferred to the Marketplaces, because you will have acquired enough funds with your first sales.

You might wonder why I am writing a

book to explain how to set up a florishing business, and help my competitors. The answer is simple : when you've been in retail for some while, you understand competition is not detrimental. When you sell the same product as your competitor, he gives you visibility, because the customer never orders instantely. He always shops around for lower prices. When your competitor advertises the same product as you, he gives you free publicity. The only war on internet is a war on prices. Whenever your competitor is out of stock, his customer will come to you.

Every day, you see new, innovative ideas or emerging start-ups, and, just a couple weeks later, several similar companies being created, because the first one work.

When a bakery shop opens in your town, and a second one opens 100 meters away, both of them manage to sell and contribute to the economy : some people will go to one of them for their own particular reason, even though prices are the same.

Competition has always existed, and does not create bankrupcies; what creates bankrupcies is innovation : creating something that doesn't exist and not being sure there is a demand for it. Because when you innovate you can never be sure, but when you re-use something that already exists , you have a lot more chances to succeed, especially if you improve it. Competition runs everybody's business, it is in no way detrimental. Someone who is walking and sees the first bakery's windows, smells its scents, might feel like buying a pastry, but, if they're lost in their thoughts, they might keep walking, until they pass by the second bakery. It's only then, they will give in to temptation. This is the perfect example of free publicity.

# ADVERTISING ON

# GOOGLE

# SHOPPING

So you started selling thanks to the

Marketplaces, and now you feel ready to

sell with your own shop, because your

working capital is now sufficient.

Here, we will not use Facebook. Even

though creating a Facebook page for

your shop is not a bad idea in itself.

Facebook ads are not a good deal. A

Facebook user isn't on Facebook to find

products. I never bought anything via

Facebook myself, and I believe you

neither, for one reason : Facebook is a

social network, not a marketplace. Users

are here for fun, not to spend money.

Facebook is a free platform, paying is not

expected on this platform, unlike Google

Shopping, where the user is looking for a

product to buy. You will reach potential

customers. Also, regarding posts on your

shop's Facebook page, for example, you have to know that Facebook uses an algorithm conceived to prevent the user from leaving the social network, therefore whenever your post countains an external link, it will be given low visibility in the News feed. Few people will see your post, whether your page has thousands of fans or not. If it was easy to reach people on Facebook, nobody would pay for ads. They are the only way to acquire traffic on Facebook, and a bad quality one at that. Facebook only works for big companies with a huge marketing budget, otherwise it's useless waste of money.

Now, to send your products to Google shopping, you will first have to create a company account on Google merchant center by using this link :

https://merchants.google.com/Signup?hl=fr&fmp=1&utm_ id=gfr&mcsubid=be-fr-z-g-mc-gfr&_ga=2.12553908.1684194687.15349 89322- 313431744.1534989322

This link is for creating an account in

France. If it doesn't work in the country you're selling to, just do an internet search for "google merchant center" and follow instructions. You will need a Gmail address to create the account. If you don't have one yet, you can create one for free, and I strongly advise you to get a new address even if you already have one.

Afterwards, you can find export modules towards Google shopping, on Prestashop addons, or, directly from your feed aggregator if you opted for one. You will have a few manipulations to do, to prove Google you are the rightful owner of your website, but everything will be explained in detail in Google's integration help, or, if you opted for a feed aggregator, their technical support will provide you will the informations you need.

As soon as your products will be imported on Google merchant center, you will have to create a Google adwords (now Google ads) account by following this link :

https://ads.google.com/um/Welcome/Ho

me?hl=fr&sourc eid=awo&subid=fr-ww-

di-g-aw-a- awhp_1!o2&sf=or&clickid=sn-

3r-or-fr-08222018&pli=1#oa

Afterwards, all you will have to do is

creating a Google shopping markting

campaign that will be linked with your

Google merchant center account, with all

your products, by setting the daily budget

you want to invest in your ads.

From there, you will start getting quality

traffic to your shop. Of course, you will

need a payment provider on your shop,

like Paypal. I personally use PayGreen,

which allows you to collect your sales one day after the order gets approved. The module is available for free on Prestashop addons. Then you will have to create an account on their website, and they will take a small fee on each one of your order, just like Paypal or any payment provider does. Prestashop will probably advice you to use Stripe as payment provider, but, when you open your account, as soon as they learn you are a Dropshipper, their bank will refuse your application, because it's still an unpopular method. Whatever your sales

turnover, their answer will be no.

# MOVING FURTHER

Dropshipping, as I explained in chapter "what is Dropshipping?", is a step, a stepping stone. There are many ways to develop Dropshipping depending on your perspectives and ambitions. If, for example, in your niche, you cannot lower your prices against your competitors and you do not want to change niche, it would be preferable to think about an alternative to Dropshipping, which is : "print on demand". This method is very efficient, because it completely removes competition.

"Print on demand" consists in creating your own products. Several societies exist in different sectors, like ShineOn, for example, which proposes customised jewelry for dropshippers. That means you are given the choice between several types of jewels, and you can customize them using your own designs, like your brand, or just designs that suit your niche. Products do not exist until your customers order them, and, when an order has been placed, the company prints your designs on the selecetd products and send them directly to your customers. This customers cannot find your product anywhere else. This is the main benefit of "print on demand" : zero competition.

Or else, after you raised your business capital with your Dropshipping sales, you could think about starting a proper retail business, by placing bulk orders and retailling them. In this case, searching for leading items and prospects interested in buying them, is necessary, but you will already know how to thanks to your experience in Dropshipping.

# CONCLUSION

Thanks to the different chapters of this book, you learnt how to prepare your online shop project in Dropshipping, you learnt how to create your shop, to evaluate your margin and benefits, to calculate your budget to succeed. You learnt to find your suppliers, how to find your products and your niche. You learnt how to open an independent business, how to pay less taxes legally, how to use Marketplaces to do your first sales, import your products, to save time.

All this will be useful to you and you will

probably not need what I'm going to offer

you now, but, to thank you for purchasing

this book, I am willing to answer your

questions, to clear any misunderstanding,

or provide you more details. Si you are

stuck on specific points, I will be inclined

to help you and answer your questions by

email at this address :

lebuzzdudropshipping@gmail.com

Good. This is where our "course" ends.

I hope you liked it and it will help you in

your project.

Do not hesitate to contact me, I will be happy to help you. This is not a book, this is a mean to share my knowledge and help those who have an ambition to succeed, this is its real goal.